Children Can Learn with their Shoes Off

a video to show good practice supporting
young people with Asperger's Syndrome in school

by

Barbara Maines

Consultants

Jo Hill
George Robinson

The title of this publication is taken from a phrase used by Rita Jordan in her
appeal to educators to be flexible in their response to the difficult physical
and sensory world experienced by people on the autistic spectrum.

ISBN-10: 1-4129-2033-7
ISBN-13: 978-1-4129-2033-9

Paul Chapman Publishing
A SAGE Publications Company
1 Oliver's Yard
55 City Road
London EC1Y 1SP

SAGE Publications Inc.
2455 Teller Road
Thousand Oaks, California 91320

SAGE Publications India Pvt Ltd
B-42, Panchsheel Enclave
Post Box 4109
New Delhi 100 017

Commissioning Editor: George Robinson
Designed and Typeset by Barbara Maines
Proofread by Wendy Ogden

© Barbara Maines 2002

Reprinted 2006

Making the video

Director, Editor and Camera	Barbara Maines
Assistant camera	Liz Isaacs
Sound	Mike Gibbs
Assistant sound	Joss Maines
	Pete Maines
	Jonathan Coles
	Hannah John

Thank you

So many teachers, support staff, parents and young people tolerated the disruption of the film crew whilst we made this video. They worked with patience and a commitment to show their best work. We are very grateful.

In the list below I have named some of the people who took part in each place that we filmed but my thanks goes to all the students, families and staff who joined in to make the task possible, and especially to the young people who showed us how their lives in school can be made easier when we try and understand.

Rita Jordan, University of Birmingham

Nita Jackson and Carolann Jackson

Chris Cottingham, Brenda Wells, Colchester Institute

Wendy Crockett, OBE, Sue Armstead, Linda Moir, Alderman Blaxill School

Pat Rogers, Alison Ball, Tricia Penfold, Claire Shiner, Chris Milson, Ilminster Avenue Nursery School

Alison Reevey, Bob Paul, Eileen Stephens, Fosse Way School

Kim McConnell, Chris Mills, St Bernadettes Primary School

Jane Sleigh, Mandy Stopard, Tina McKeoun, Backwell Comprehensive School

David Cropp, Bartley Green Technology College

Darren Barton, Bearwood Primary School

Jenny Bentall, Claudette Cole, Jan Elliott, Waverley School

Jo Hill, Phil O'Donohue, Louise Amos, Julie Davies, Ben Higgins, Alison Dollin, Kingsweston School

Tracy Cavalier, City of Bristol College

Contents

Introduction by Barbara Maines

Lucky Duck has built its training and publications reputation on a self-concept approach to the management of behaviour and learning and this road has led us into many related fields: Bullying, Emotional Literacy, Circle Time, Parenting. Most of our publications are written by practising teachers whose work we have supported. We have always agreed that we would only accept for publication material which was familiar to us and congruent with our own philosophy.

In 1999 Clare Sainsbury attended a Lucky Duck Course and talked with the trainer about her experience. She has Asperger's Syndrome. At our invitation she went on to write the award winning book Martian in the Playground and introduced us to a whole new perspective on autistic spectrum disorder. Her expertise and her direct personal writing turned this academic book into an entrancing read, a book that you can't put down.

During the year that this book was in preparation I directed the video 'Special Needs and the Literacy Hour', DfEE 2000. In one of the schools we filmed a boy with Asperger's Syndrome. His talented teacher and support staff had devised an extensive programme of visual signs which allowed him to understand the routine of his school day, conform to many required behavioural expectations and maintain a relatively calm and confident approach to school life. It was unexpected and remarkable to observe the responses of the rest of the class... all the children used the visual signals and this meant that information and instructions were presented in verbal and visual modality. This seemed to work for all the children without an apparent struggle to read difficult words. Because the symbols and signs are clear and representational the comprehension seemed to be simultaneous with the spoken word. I was struck by the potential benefits to children with any sort of language, communication or social difficulty. It was an example of integration at its best.

We do not claim to be specialists in Asperger's Syndrome or Autistic Spectrum Disorder but the inspiration from Clare's book and a realisation that this is a common and often undiagnosed condition spurred us on to learn more. Our intention was not to become experts in the field but to focus on ways in which our experience of good classroom practice could be extended and adapted to support young people with Asperger's Syndrome whilst enriching the experience of the whole class.

I attended some courses, talked to experts, bought some books and spent some time on specialist websites and quickly discovered that, without a prohibitive amount of time and expenditure, teachers can adopt a range of strategies which can significantly improve the classroom and social experience of school for young people with the condition and incidentally for many of their peers.

All of the courses presented interesting information and perspectives but one particular experience was especially valuable and that was the one day course by Rita Jordan from Birmingham University. Her approach is theoretical, practical and intensely humane and we are very grateful to her for the time she gave to film an interview – part of which is included in the video, and the full transcript of which is printed in this publication. Her knowledge and attitude played a significant part in our motivation to make this video and we are very grateful for her support and encouragement.

A young woman inspired by Clare Sainsbury's book sent us her own manuscript which she wrote when she was only eighteen. It turned out to be a huge document – a personal and intensely moving account of her experience as a young person with Asperger's Syndrome, intertwined with a poetic and dramatic novel. It was clear to us that half of the book was a possible Lucky Duck publication but that this would have to be dissected out – a major editing task. The author is Nita Jackson and I set off to visit her at her home in Essex. I met Nita at her home and she wrote the music for the video during our visit, setting one of her poems to her own composition. Nita took a month to complete the edit and submitted her shortened manuscript, 'Standing Down, Falling Up' which we published in 2002.

People with Asperger's Syndrome struggle to manage everyday social communication for reasons which are explained in the definition of the condition. They may experience intense distress which is sometimes exhibited in a range of difficult, challenging and upsetting behaviours. There isn't a magic key to turn which will make it easier for them and for those who parent and teach them... rather a range of adjustments and interventions, each with a bit of understanding, a changed way of interacting, an extra bit of flexibility, a technique which seems to contradict 'common sense'. In making this video we have visited teachers who have used or devised the strategies and filmed them with the young people.

We are immensely grateful to the teachers and the young people for their generous commitment to this venture. Filming is always disruptive – it is naïve to pretend otherwise. For young people with Asperger's Syndrome any disruption to routine, any uncertainty is especially difficult and often provokes extreme anxiety. Working with the young people who participated in this video, observing their conscientious efforts to help us get what we needed, was very moving. During one stressful episode I asked a young man if I was upsetting him. He replied, "Yes, you are actually." I apologised and tried to find an easier way to direct that scene. He spent the rest of the day apologising to me for his 'outburst'. Our only excuse for causing this distress was that, in making and distributing the video, we hope that many teachers, young people and their families will find some confirmation of existing good practice and some new ideas to add to their repertoire.

Because one of the characteristics of the conditions is an inability to feel or reflect upon a situation from another person's point of view, people with Asperger's Syndrome are described as lacking in empathy. It is certainly true that the communication difficulties can severely impair their ability to accurately read the signs associated with emotion, but they do understand feelings and can be extremely sensitive towards other people when awareness is facilitated. The positive aspect of this difficulty in thinking and feeling in another person's shoes is that they lack guile, they are not devious because they do not invent a deception or a trick with the other person's understanding in mind.

This straightforwardness is engaging and endearing. Working with the young people who feature on this video was a very positive experience for the crew – thank you.

What does the video show?

During our learning process we met teachers and parents who told us about ways in which children with Asperger's Syndrome were understood, supported and encouraged. The video clips have been grouped into sections and each one is tagged with a number on a different coloured background. This is to help you find your way around the tape when searching. For each section there is some writing and some references to help you study the topic further.

Section 1	green	Who and what are we studying?
Section 2	peach	Awareness and flexibility
Section 3	blue	Visual cues – structured (PECS)
Section 4	lilac	Non-verbal communication and photographs
Section 5	lemon	Social stories
Section 6	orange	Feelings and emotions
Section 7	grey	Drama and social skills
Section 8	beige	Follow up work
Section 9	white	Friendship and support
Section 10	pink	Relaxation
Section 11	mauve	Adolescence
Section 12	red	Special skills - savantisn

In addition to the filming we did in mainstream schools there are two sections filmed in special schools and one in a nursery where we were able to demonstrate some strategies that do involve some extra training and/or preparation, but which will easily transfer to a mainstream setting, especially where a young person has additional support.

What the publication does not provide

Because this video handbook does not attempt to provide the reader with a textbook on Asperger's Syndrome/Autistic Spectrum Disorder, it might be helpful to draw your attention to some useful books and websites which will be of interest to those who wish to study the subject in more detail.

These can be found towards the end of the book on page 33.

The video

Each section of the video is described on the following pages. You will find a summary of the content for that section and some references of resources where appropriate.

Section 1

Who and what are we studying?

In this section of the video Rita Jordan explains what Asperger's Syndrome is and her presentation is punctuated by some comments from Nita Jackson, author of Standing Down, Falling Up. See the transcript of Rita's interview for a full text for this section - page22.

The triad of impairment

Autism is a complex condition that disrupts the most central aspects of human life. It is characterised by abnormalities, difficulties and differences in:

the development of communication skills
the development of social relationships
and the presence of marked obsessive and repetitive behaviour.

Beginning in infancy, the condition appears to have a genetic basis, although the relevant genes have yet to be identified. Also associated with learning difficulties, autism is considered to be one of the most severe of the developmental disorders.

Frequency

At least one and maybe as many as six children in every 1000 are affected by an autism spectrum disorder. It is a condition with wide ranging degrees of severity (hence the phrase autistic spectrum). At one end of the spectrum are children who seem totally cut off from the social world. They may have no language, or may have the technical aspects of language but fail to use these for normal communication. At the other end of the spectrum are individuals with Asperger's Syndrome. Their social and communication problems are more subtle, but are still severe and are accompanied by an insensitivity to normal social cues, as well as difficulties in social interaction.

Individuals with Asperger's Syndrome, which is thought to be more common than autism, typically have no associated language delay in childhood, and may be of normal or even above normal intelligence.

Whilst education, care and therapeutic approaches can help people with autism maximise their potential, impairments in social and communication skills may persist throughout life.

Family life is often disrupted by unpredictable behaviour problems and this causes high levels of stress for parents and carers as they attempt to encourage their child's social development.

Despite several decades of research, relatively little is understood about the causes of autism and there is currently no cure for the condition.

Section 2

Awareness and flexibility

During our search for good practice we met many members of schools and college staff who made significant adjustments and planned brilliant strategies. This section does not show any of the formal or published interventions. It is a collection of individual examples of good practice which has made life in school so much better for the young people involved. For example David Copp is talking with a student who finds eye contact very difficult and uncomfortable. To allow the young man to look at his face with ease David takes his gaze away from the student for periods of time during the conversation.

In this section there are no 'formal' strategies to observe but look out for flexibility and special consideration from teachers, support staff and peers.

Section 3

Visual cues – structured (PECS)

In this section of the video we see structured symbols used as a communication system. When first introduced the 'Picture Exchange Communication System' (PECS) is used with one adult, the trainer, and the response to the symbol guarantees an appropriate response.

As the child becomes familiar with the system and especially where integration into mainstream school is planned, the PECS activity may be linked with language. In this piece of video Harry is working with his teacher and his LSA and he uses language to support the communication he has already achieved with the symbol card. Harry now uses the PECS exchange with other adults and children in the class but makes very little eye-contact during these exchanges.

The Picture Exchange Communication System (PECS) was developed 12 years ago as a unique alternative training package that allows children and adults with autism and other communication deficits to initiate communication. First used at the Delaware Autistic Program, PECS has received worldwide recognition for focusing on the initiation component of communication. PECS does not require complex or expensive materials. It was created with educators, resident care providers and families in mind, and so it is readily used in a variety of settings.

PECS begins with teaching a student to exchange a picture of a desired item with a teacher, who immediately honours the request. Verbal prompts are not used, thus building immediate initiation and avoiding prompt dependency. The system goes on to teach discrimination of symbols and then puts them all together in simple "sentences". Children are also taught to comment and answer direct questions. Many preschoolers using PECS also begin developing speech.

Visual Timetables

The PECS approach supports the use of symbols or photographs to sequence events. The use of schedules with the more able young person can enhance the independence of the individual and lead then to being able to carry out a number of activities without reference back to the adult. Symbol timetables offer all class members a non-verbal system for predicting the order of events in the day.

Frost, L. and Bondy, A. (1994)
PECS training manual
Available in the UK from Pyramid Educational Consultants UK Ltd
www.pecs.com
01273 728888
The manual is most useful when read in conjunction with training. If it is felt that a young person may benefit from using PECs then an appropriate starting point may be an LEA advisory team or the young person's speech and language therapist.

Section 4
Non-verbal communication

This section of the video shows some strategies for informal use of visual support for learning.

The use of photos and symbols can enhance learning across the curriculum. Some young people on the autistic spectrum find it difficult to match the real object with line drawn symbols and for this reason the increased use of photographs in school with instant printing of digital images is a great advantage.

It is important to note that some students fail to generalise from a photo, for example only accept red balls if this is on the photo whereas the teacher may be referencing balls in general. The way the materials are used must suit the abilities of the particular student.

Photos or symbols can be used in a huge variety of situations to give the student visual cues. Some examples are....

- A photo book to prepare for transition to another school
- Holiday brochures, leaflets of tourist attractions to familiarise the young person with where they are going to reduce anxiety
- Family changes illustrated in a photo or life story book. Helping a young person to cope with a death in the family, a new baby, etc.
- In school it may be helpful to have a photo board of staff or of pupils in the class
- In lessons photographs can help students understand new vocabulary, for example when talking about other countries or cultures

Section 5
Social Stories

Another way for young people to rehearse activities, look at worrying issues and work towards an appropriate response to these is to use social stories.

By creating a picture or written guide the young person can approach a situation with an acquired level of emotional knowledge, through discussion to enable them to practise responses to the experience.

Social stories are written in specific language and are personalised to the young person in a specific situation, for example coping with a change, dealing with something which makes them anxious.

For Ritchie on the video, the concerns were the physical changes happening to him as he went through puberty, which had led on to concern about moving from school to college and becoming an adult. This was particularly upsetting for Ritchie as the adult he felt closest to, his grandfather, had died. Thus Ritchie was anxious that growing up was exposing him to the unknown and also to death.

In most situations social stories are written with an individual. At times if the issues are relevant to a small group then to increase cooperation skills and empathy other pupils can be brought in. Even though other pupils are assisting, the focus is on Ritchie's situation but some of the discussion may spark recognition of similar feelings or experiences across the group.

Social stories have been researched and devised by Carol Gray and training is available for school staff and parents.

The Carol Gray Centre website provides a clear description of her development of the Social Story process. It can be found at

www.TheGrayCenter.org

Gray, C. 2000
Writing Social Stories with Carol Gray
Future Horizons – available in the UK from Winslow Press
www.winslow-press.co.uk
This is a video workshop with accompanying workbook.

Carol Gray began using social stories in 1991 to address a difficulty of a 6 year old boy who was finding inclusion into his mainstream class' PE lesson very difficult. Since then the techniques have been revised and the workbook and video provide an explanation of the theory and practice of writing social stories.

Section 6
Feelings and emotions

In this section of the video we see the progressive work being done, over several years, to offer young people with Asperger's Syndrome the opportunity to improve their ability to understand and observe the emotions expressed by other people.

Asperger's young people have a full range of feelings and emotions and are many of the things that make them happy, sad, anxious, are felt in the same way, and sometimes even more intensely than the rest of us. Their difficulty with understanding feelings and therefore with empathic or socially appropriate responses lies in their inability to read the signals expressed by others, and to imagine themselves in the place of the other person.

At an intellectual level people with Asperger's Syndrome do understand that others can suffer the same range of emotions that they themselves experience… but they don't sense it intuitively or by observation. Like so many social reactions it has to be consciously considered.

As well as teaching this as a skill, the reasons for it are explained and whether the student then chooses to use the skill depends upon a conscious intention. As with many skills the ability to make appropriate use of them will also depend upon the stress levels experienced at the time.

It is this process of having to approach several different tasks separately: listen to the words, watch and interpret the face, consider the meanings, that makes communication so stressful and difficult. Helping young people manage these situations better depends upon their understanding of the task and long and repeated opportunities to practise the activities.

NB Warning. When role-playing or pretending emotions it is important to make sure that the young people are able to move out of that state and back to a calm mood at the end of the lesson.

A useful resource for this work is described below.

Mind Reading – the interactive guide to emotions

Developed by Baron-Cohen and his team at Cambridge University

The information below is taken from the website
www.human-emotions.com
and described in an article by Dea Birkett, G2 section of the Guardian September 3rd 2002 which can be read on www.guardian.co.uk

Mind Reading is a unique reference work covering the entire spectrum of human emotions. Using the software you can explore over 400 emotions, seeing and hearing each one performed by six different people.

Mind Reading is for everyone interested in emotions. It has been designed with awareness of the special needs of children and adults who have recognising emotional expression in others. It is also an invaluable resource for actors, directors, writers and anyone involved in the dramatic arts. The title enables the user to study emotions and to learn the meanings of facial expressions and tone of voice, drawing on a comprehensive underlying audio-visual and text database.

Mind Reading consists of three main applications:

 ✛ Emotions Library – reference guide

 ✛ Learning Centre – quizzes and lessons

 ✛ Games Zone – fun learning activities

A fourth application is available for tailoring the software to the specific needs of individual users, and for monitoring user performance.

Another important consideration to consider when planning the social teaching programme for young people with Asperger's Syndrome is to understand the theory of mind.

Theory of Mind

Does the autistic child have a 'theory of mind'?
Baron-Cohen, S., Leslie, A.M. & Frith, U. (1985).
www.garysturt.free-online.co.uk/baron.htm

In past years autism was attributed to poor parenting and family interactions but these blameful explanations have been rejected and conclusively proved to be unfounded. Simon Baron Cohen et al at Cambridge University present the absence of 'Theory of Mind' as defining the nature of Autism. A simple test of social cognition called the Sally-Anne test devised by Wimmer and Perner, 1983, can establish the presence or absence of Theory of Mind.

1. Children are tested individually, seated at a desk opposite to an experimenter.

2. Two dolls are shown, Sally and Anne. Sally has a basket in front of her and Anne has a box.

3. After being told the names of the dolls, the children are asked to confirm that they remember the names.

4. Sally places a marble in her basket and goes for a walk (disappears from view).

5. Whilst Sally is away, Anne plays a trick and takes the marble from Sally's basket and transfers it to her (Anne's) box.

6. Sally returns.

7. The child is asked the main experimental question (the 'belief' question). "Where will Sally look for her marble?"

8. The correct response is "in Sally's basket", because that is where Sally left it, and she is unaware of Anne's trickery.

Without a 'Theory of Mind' subjects will make the incorrect response, "in Anne's box". This is because the young person with autism fails to understand that the experimenter wants them to 'put themselves in someone else's shoes', they can relay the information they themselves know but fail to see the situation from the perspective of Sally. However it is worth noting that with appropriate input some young people with Asperger's Syndrome can do this.

Section 7
Drama and social skills

This section of the video concentrates on a group of young people in their final year of school. They have been visiting the local college once a week, working with Tracy Cavalier, a drama teacher/drama therapist to develop the skills they will need to manage their social life and learning when they transfer after the summer term. The video was made on the last day of school, showing the end-result of months of practice and personal development. The programme of work and rationale are discussed below in a contribution from Tracy Cavalier.

The video sequence we see is the result of a whole year's work during which the young people have developed the various activities: telling news in turns and listening to each other, making eye contact when passing objects or preparing to speak, moving about comfortably, sharing the space in the room.

The students take their break in the canteen where they choose food, pay for it and sit with other people. All these skills have been taught and practised week by week, in preparation for transfer to college after they leave school.

Miming to favourite songs gives students the opportunity to perform in front of their peers and to copy body language and gesture. It is a great boost to their confidence and provides an age-appropriate experience for teenagers. In addition the audience are practising giving their attention to the performance and showing their appreciation. This part of the session evolved from one student's particular interest and several others wanted to join in.

After each session in college the students reinforce their learning with their class-teacher, back in school. It is important to watch sections 7 and 8 together.

Kingsweston School and City of Bristol College link programme

The aim of the project at the start was to provide a safe space in which the pupils could get used to a college environment in preparation for leaving school at the end of the academic year. Drama would provide an opportunity to explore and express their feelings around this issue as well as a forum for rehearsal of social and communication skills. As the facilitator of the group my main concern was to build the pupils' confidence and self-esteem and trust that from a position of increased self-confidence they would feel more able to make a smooth transition from school to college. I did not have a set curriculum to follow nor were there any formal assessment criteria to be achieved. Specific learning objectives were entirely open. I decided that the focus of the sessions would be on exploration rather than achievement.

In agreement with Carl Rogers, I feel very strongly that in order to learn we need to feel valued and accepted. In my experience, if an educator focuses on pointing out where and how a learner should be different from how they are now they will probably dig their heels in and get stuck in that place, unable to learn because of a sub-conscious defence of their current position. If, on the other hand, we focus on a sincere, genuine and empathic process of uncovering where the learner is at any particular moment, through gentle enquiry, and then communicate acceptance and 'prizing' of them wherever they are, then they are less likely to feel attacked and will be less likely to erect defences. They will probably become more open to trying out new ways of being and new behaviours and will be more open to learning and developing. I feel that any other approach inhibits rather than promotes the growth of self-esteem, which is now widely acknowledged as the starting point for all learning.

I was therefore keen that the sessions focus on what the learners *could* do rather than what they couldn't do, and that a non-judgemental atmosphere be created. I wanted to get to know them in a gentle and gradual way. Above all I wanted to make them feel safe, and I did this by following the above principles as well as through the provision of a clear, simple and repeated structure to the classes and by presenting myself in as congruent a way as I could.

Sessions took place on a Thursday morning between 0950 and 1215. Getting used to the canteen was a very important learning objective for the group, so it was important that we took a break half way through.

Sessions were structured into Arrival, Warm-Up, Development and Closure phases. We took a break between 1100 and 1120. When everyone was present there were a total of eleven people in the room: myself, eight learners (7 boys and 1 girl), their class teacher and their teaching assistant. The other two members of staff were very much part of the group, taking part in activities and providing one to one support when necessary.

To begin with I proposed activities appropriate to each phase. (As time went on the group became more and more pro-active and in control of the sessions themselves.) These activities were mostly presented as invitations and I made sure to communicate that no activity was compulsory and that it was perfectly ok to sit out and just watch, the role of the audience in drama being as important as that of the performer. This gave individuals a chance to contact their feelings around a given activity, to acknowledge and accept those feelings, to monitor how they developed and to decide for themselves when and if they felt ok to take part. In this way they learnt about taking care of themselves and about taking personal responsibility.

Activities were carefully 'laddered' in terms of the amount of risk-taking that was required in order to do them; we started off easily and gently and moved gradually into the more challenging ones. I tried to evolve these as smoothly as possible from their predecessors, building all the time on what had been achieved and slowly adding natural developments, rather than jumping from one activity to the next. This gentle lead-in is always important with drama, which is a powerful medium and can be frightening for anyone, but it is even more important when working with sensitive groups such as this.

I was also open to any suggestions that the group may have had. There was an ethos of trying to involve everyone in the decision about whether or not we would try a suggested activity, and an ethos of experimentation and risk-taking; of it being ok for something not to work out. In this way the group evolved their own activities which were then practised and developed over time and they took great pride and enjoyment in what they created.

All the way through I practised positive teaching methods, noticing and paying attention to the things that were going well, to celebrating an individual's achievement, however small, and to ignoring as far as possible any negative behaviour. I was absolutely determined never to 'tell anyone off'. This did not mean that I condoned inappropriate behaviour or did not challenge certain view-points that were expressed. But this was done in a spirit of enquiry and curiosity, and I tried never to present myself as being the one who was automatically right by virtue of my position of power as leader of the group. Although, technically speaking, this was education, not therapy, I nevertheless tried to practise 'unconditional positive regard' (Murray Cox). I do not feel, at the end of the day, that when they are practised with integrity and skill there is really that much difference between the two disciplines of therapy and education, both of them being, as they are, essentially about learning.

There was also an ethos of students working out problems for themselves rather than being told what to do or provided with answers by me. Conflicts were not swept under the carpet but were confronted and discussed and we tried to work with rather than against behaviours, even if that meant taking a conscious decision to ignore them.

The results were very positive and the project has been a great success. All eight of the students applied to come to this particular college and as a result a new programme of courses has been created for them. They have enjoyed the sessions a great deal, as have I. There have been many magical moments, much joy and much 'coming out of shells'. And also some difficult moments. We have decided to continue working together as a group for another year, and that is something that I am looking forward to doing tremendously, and I am grateful for the continuing opportunity to work with and learn from what I consider to be a very special group of people.

Tracy Cavalier. July 2002.

Tracy Cavalier is state registered Dramatherapist who works mainly through the City of Bristol College Faculty of Vocational Preparation and Progression. She is available for consultation, training, teaching, therapeutic drama work and Dramatherapy for groups and individuals.

Drama and social skills resources

There are a number of practical workbooks available on social skills development, many offering a worksheet approach.

Schroeder, A. (2000)
Socially speaking – a pragmatic social skills programme for primary pupils
LDA. Duke Street . Wisbech . Cambridgeshire . PE13 2AE
www.ldalearning.com

Most of the resources in this book are photocopiable and are relevant to the slightly older pupil with Asperger's Syndrome.

Peeters, T. (1997)
Autism – From theoretical understanding to educational intervention
WHURR publishers
www.whurr.co.uk

The author of this book regards autistic people as "hyperrealist" in a world of "surrealism" we call normal. Having a literal mind has profound consequences for the development of communication, social behaviour and emotional maturity, and for the ability to enjoy leisure time. This study provides a theoretical understanding of autism, to help carers adapt to the autistic person's thought processes. It also offers practical intervention strategies for education and treatment. It is illustrated with numerous quotes from parents and autistic people, providing insights into the condition. The chapter on social interactions in this text is very detailed and is of interest to those wishing for a more in depth understanding of this area.

Sherratt, D. and Peter, M. (2002)
Developing play and drama in children with autistic spectrum disorders
David Fulton
www.fultonbooks.co.uk

This work clearly explains the theory on which the authors' practice is based. The book looks at the benefits of play and the development of play skills. It gives detail on the use of drama as a curriculum tool and also as a medium to address some of the difficulties arising from the triad of impairments.

Section 8
Follow up work

During the follow up session the young people can talk through any issues raised. This establishes a link from the drama session at college into the social skills curriculum within the school. In the classroom setting the class teacher can further develop the skills and refer back to other parts of the social skills curriculum. It is vital when working with young people on the autistic spectrum that skills can be practised in different situations and can be built upon and developed with frequent opportunity for repetition and reinforcement within the curriculum.

In this section we see the young people back in school, following up the morning activities in college. The two sections are closely linked and without this follow up work it is less likely that the students would:

+ Understand the meaning of the skills and activities they have learned

+ Be able to generalise them to other situations

The achievements are the result of the learning that has taken place over several years and the relationship that they have with their teacher supports their feelings of safety and their ability to try new skills. It is also interesting to observe how well they respond to each other's success, having learned ways to show appreciation and to give praise.

Section 9
Friendship and support

Many young people with Asperger's Syndrome long for friendship and suffer from loneliness and sometimes from bullying. In this section of the video we see how support and friendships are encouraged for young people with Asperger's Syndrome.

"Here is one of my most vivid memories of school: I am standing in a corner of the playground as usual, as far away as possible from people who might bump into me or shout, gazing into the sky and absorbed in my own thoughts. I am eight or nine years old and have begun to realise that I am different in some nameless but all-pervasive way.

I don't understand the children around me. They frighten and confuse me. They don't want to talk about things that are interesting. I used to think that they were silly, but now I am beginning to understand that I am the one who is all wrong. I try so hard to do what I am told, but just when I think I am being most helpful and good, the teachers tell me off and I don't know why. It's as if everybody is playing some complicated game and I am the only one who hasn't been told the rules. But no-one will admit that it's a game or that there are rules, let alone explain them to me. Maybe it's all a joke being played on me; I know about "jokes". I would be happy if they left me alone to think my thoughts, but they won't.

I think that I might be an alien who has been put on this planet by mistake; I hope that this is so, because this means that there might be other people out there in the universe like me. I dream that one day a spaceship will fall from the sky onto the tarmac in front of me, and the people who step out of the spaceship will tell me, "It's all been a dreadful mistake. You were never meant to be here. We are your people and now we've come to take you home."

Sainsbury, C. 2000

Young people with Asperger's Syndrome may appear 'different' in several ways. Not only do they struggle with the rhythms of social interaction, turn-taking and acknowledgments, but they may also move in an awkward way and demonstrate particular routines or obsessions which get in the way of friendships. Just as adults can respond with understanding and adjust their expectations, so can young people when given the opportunity.

Self-esteem and respect

Adults can model positive appreciation of the achievements of students with Asperger's Syndrome, especially when they have particular talents or specialised knowledge. In the video we see some examples of this when students admire the model made by a student gifted in construction and exlectronics.

Another pupil is a very talented artist and he shares his techniques with some friends who learn to draw some of his invented characters. This has been a great boost to his popularity in school.

Circle of Friends

Circle of Friends is an established intervention which draws upon the support of the peers to make life easier and promote inclusion for a young person with any sort of difficulty. During a series of meetings a small group of peers are encouraged to be empathic and altruistic and to plan their own positive interventions. Young people who might otherwise have rejected or ignored, or even worse, bullied a young person with Asperger's Syndrome are motivated to help and support.

For young people with social and communication difficulties a visual representation of the circle of friendship surrounding the young person is especially helpful to support the verbal discussion.

Where the focus on a particular child might be difficult the same supportive behaviours and tolerance of differences can be encouraged by using an imaginary character or by raising awareness in Circle Time sessions. This can then be developed into Circle of Friends sessions for a named student.

Axup, T. E. J., (1996)
The Circle of Friends Process: A life changing experience?
Unpublished M.Ed. Dissertation.
Faculty of Education, University of the West of England
www.uwe.ac.uk/library

Forest, M., and Pearpoint, J., (1992)
Commonsense tools: maps and circles. Inclusion Papers
Inclusion Press
www.inclusion.com/PI-CIRCLES.OF.FRIENDS.html

Mackan, P., and Cormier, R., (1992)
Dynamics of support circles Inclusion Papers
Inclusion Press
www.inclusion.com/PI-CIRCLES.OF.FRIENDS.html

Maines, B. and Robinson, G. (1998)
All for Alex, a circle of friends training video
Lucky Duck Publishing
www.luckyduck.co.uk

Newton, C., and Wilson, D., (1996)
A Circle of Friends
Special Children (January)
www.education-quest.com

Newton, C., Tailor, G., and Wilson, D., (1996)
Circle of Friends: an inclusive approach to meeting emotional and behavioural needs
Educational Psychology in Practice 4 (January)
www.tandf.co.uk/journals/carfax

Snow, J., and Forest, M., (1987)
Circles, in: M Forest (ed.) More Education/Integration
G Allen Roeher Institute

Section 10
Relaxation and Scripted Fantasy

In the video a mixture of resources from the two texts below are used in the sea shell session with the pupils relaxing on the floor. To extend this work the pupils have regular weekly yoga sessions which also have an emphasis on breath control and body awareness.

The purpose of offering relaxation techniques to students with ASD is related to the very high anxiety levels which is common for many of these young people.

As with many skills though for some students with autism the ability to transfer these skills into different situations can be a difficult road to travel.

The purpose of linking this to guided fantasy / imaginative work is to allow pupils to further explore this part of the triad. There are many young people with Asperger's Syndrome who have very detailed imaginary worlds which seem to be used to block out what's happening around them. The addition of guided fantasy to the curriculum is hoped to allow these particular students to look beyond their own imaginings.

For other young people the skill of calming themselves is an incredibly important step on the way to learning self-management of their own behaviours, this leads to increased independence from adult support.

The social and communication difficulties experienced by young people with Asperger's Syndrome make forming and keeping friendships difficult. Social interaction is stressful, the sensory world can be disabling and there is often a steady build up of stress and anxiety during the day. Some parents report that a son or daughter will manage to hold it together at school but on returning home there may be prolonged disturbance as the child relaxes.

Structured periods of relaxation can be built into the timetable and once the skills are learned they can be re-created in a few minutes. Jo Hill uses a scripted fantasy with her students, to achieve a positive and relaxed mood. Alison Reevey follows up the relaxation and breathing with a technique to 'fix' the relaxed state. By making the individual hand movements the young people associate this with their good, calm feeling, and can bring it back at another time by repeating the hand movement.

Stone, M. K. (1995)
Don't just do something, sit there – developing children's spiritual awareness.
RMEP
www.scm-canterburypress.co.uk

Beesley, M. (1990)
"Stilling" – a pathway for spiritual learning in the national curriculum.
Salisbury Diocesan Board of Education

Section 11

Adolescence

This section of the video is filmed on visits to college to see how older students are supported in further education establishments. For some the opportunity to join social activities with their peers is an aspiration and all the examples are based on careful planning, rehearsing an event and reviewing the experience afterwards. It is important that the young people give informed consent to these events and that they choose behaviours which will help them to achieve their own goals.

Section 12

Special Skills - Savantism

In this section of the video we see some young people with special or extraordinary skills, and consider whether they are of practical use or can be identified to encourage esteem from peers.

Some young people with Asperger's Syndrome are especially gifted in a particular skill, talent or intelligence. Savant skills occur within a narrow but constant range of human mental functions, generally in six areas: calendar calculating; lightening calculating & mathematical ability; art (drawing or sculpting); music (usually piano with perfect pitch); mechanical abilities; and spatial skills. In some instances unusual language abilities have been reported but those are rare. Other skills much less frequently reported include map memorising, visual measurement, extrasensory perception, unusual sensory discrimination such as enhanced sense of touch & smell, and perfect appreciation of passing time without knowledge of a clock face. The most common savant skill is musical ability. A regularly re-occurring triad of musical genius, blindness and autism is particularly striking in the world literature on this topic.

Premature birth history is commonly reported in persons with Savant Syndrome.

In some cases of Savant Syndrome a single special skill exists; in others there are several skills co-existing simultaneously. The skills tend to be right hemisphere in type – non-symbolic, artistic, concrete, directly perceived – in contrast to left hemisphere type that tend to be more sequential, logical, and symbolic including language specialisation.

Whatever the special skills, they are always linked with phenomenal memory. That memory, however, is a special type – very narrow but exceedingly deep – within its narrow confines. Such memory is a type of "unconscious reckoning" – habit or procedural memory – which relies on more primitive circuitry (cortico-striatal) than higher level (cortico-limbic) cognitive or associative memory used more commonly and regularly in normal persons. Approximately 10% of persons with Autistic Disorder have some savant skills or specially developed abilities.

An excellent website with lots of information and articles about savantism is provided by Winsconsin Medical School

www.wisconsinmedicalsociety.org/savant/aspergers.cfm

Transcript of the interview with Rita Jordan

Dr. Rita Jordan
Senior Lecturer in autistic spectrum disorders
School of Education, University of Birmingham

A few short extracts from the interview with Rita Jordan are featured in the video. The full text is transcribed below.

What is Asperger's syndrome?

Children and young people with Asperger's syndrome suffer from one of the autistic spectrum disorders. It is named after Hans Asperger and it is a 'hard g' not a 'soft g' which some people get confused about. He was identifying Autism almost at the same time as Kanner was doing so in America. Hans Asperger was writing in German in the middle of the Second World War, so his work really wasn't known about until Lorna Wing bought it to our attention in 1981, and later in 1991 Utta Frith translated his seminal paper. Because he became interested in a group of young men who were more able than groups that Kanner described then his name has become associated with that group. So we now use Asperger's Syndrome and it appears now as a separate diagnostic category and we use it for someone who has an autistic spectrum disorder and therefore shares the triad of impairments which is the triad that Lorna Wing first identified but who does not have a structural language problem that means that they should be able to speak in sentences but will still have the communication problems that are associated with autism, nor should they have any significant learning disability. They may have particular parts of specific learning problems but they shouldn't have any general cognitive deficit.

Triad of impairment

Lorna Wing and her colleague Judith Gould first identified what she termed as a triad, three areas of social impairment. It is important to remember that she was talking about a social impairment. It is also important to remember that she was talking about areas of development rather than particular behaviours. Behaviours which are themselves autistic or Asperger like. People with Asperger's Syndrome do just the same things as we all do, but they may do them to the extreme and they may be very ordinary circumstances, which wouldn't be stressful for us but are stressful for them and therefore they respond in a particular way. Never the less there are areas of development that are affected and that's why they get areas of difficulty, disability and stress.

<u>1. Areas of communication - that is all forms of communication.</u>

Autism and the whole range of autistic spectrum disorders are the only conditions in which language development and communication development are separate. That means that you can get, as you do in Asperger's Syndrome, someone who develops speech at or soon after the normal age for doing so and may speak in fact much better than his contempories, much better than his peers. He may have very adult language. I say he because predominately we are talking about boys although there are some girls with Asperger's Syndrome. But even though he has good speech, he may not know how to use it properly, he may not be able to understand it at the level which he can say it which of course it very confusing for people talking to him and he may not understand any of the other features that go along with language that help us to interact with what it means. Because when we listen to someone speaking we don't just listen to what the words mean, what the sentences mean, we don't just use our knowledge of English grammar and vocabulary, we actually try to work out, all the time that we are listening what the person means. To use Bruner's phrase, we go beyond the information given, we try to work out why they are saying things, and the context we take into account in order to interpret what is meant. The person with Asperger's Syndrome cannot do any of these things or may only learn to do so very slowly and painfully. In the beginning, their approach to understanding language is to try desperately to understand, quite literally, what those words and sentences mean. If you say "Take the Register to the office", the boy with Asperger's Syndrome will happily bring it back again. Then, when the teacher gets very upset and says "I thought I told you to take it to the office" the boy is bewildered because he did so. It just never occurred to him to think "Why is she asking me to take it to the office?" "Is it normal to take a register for a walk?" He's just thinking "This is what she told me to do" and he does it exactly, but no more than what he's told. It's not just the words and language. It's the things that go with it, the facial expressions which can alter the meaning, the tone of voice – many children with Asperger's Syndrome struggle to realise that things said in an angry voice, said harshly, shouted are the same as the things whispered in a soft and friendly manner so they may be very distracted by the tone in which the language is used. Equally they don't understand that if you wink or raise an eyebrow you may change the meaning of what you said. They can hear the intonation patterns and we know that a few of them who start off their understanding the language through echolalia may even reproduce those intonation patterns exactly but when they come to use their own spontaneous speech we find far less use of intonation patterns.

We find, in fact, that many of them speak in monotones or they may have a very singsong, exaggerated, peculiar form of intonation because what they are picking up is that they can understand intonation patterns but they don't know what those stresses mean. They don't know the implications; they don't know why one part of the word is stressed and not another or why one word in a sentence is stressed and not another. So again all these things distract from the meaning of what they are attending to. Of course, they will depend on the child being able to attend.

Many people with Autism and Asperger's Syndrome are unaware of what active listening means. They have no sense of how to listen, of how to take meaning from what they listen to and therefore how to retain it and use it in their conversations. Someone may be using very good language when they are giving a lecture, even though they may be talking to somebody in effect that is often what they are doing is giving a kind of lecture but that for them is easier than trying to have a conversation. Easier than recognising when the pauses are, easier than knowing how to give pauses/allow for the natural breaks are so that other people can come in to the conversation. So for them very often it is easier to try to hold the floor and try to speak at people rather than listen to people. The problem is of course that if we are faced with someone without language, or with a very clear language difficulty then we are naturally triggered to adjust. We slow down, we speak in shorter sentences and we recognise that the person has a problem in communicating with us but when we are faced with someone with Asperger's Syndrome who is talking to us nineteen to a dozen right in our faces often using very obscure and grown-up language we are not triggered to think that this is a language problem, we are not triggered to think that the child does not understand. Instead we are driven to think that the child has a behaviour difficulty, that the child is deliberately being difficult and so we don't adjust our language and we misinterpret how the child is responding.

2. Social understanding

The second area of the triad is perhaps the most fundamental area, is the area of social understanding and development. It's not just a matter of children with Asperger's Syndrome not having social skills. If it were a matter of not having social skills the problem would be relatively simple because we could just teach them. There are many other reasons why children may not develop social skills including, of course, a background in which those are not very important or different from the mainstream and they are not taught those skills. Children with Asperger's Syndrome fundamentally don't understand social interaction; they don't understand the social and emotional basis of social interaction.

Because of that, they don't develop their social skills and because of that, it's extremely difficult to teach social skills without that underpinning understanding. If we just approach it from teaching a missing social skill, if we teach to deficits if you like, the child is often made more disabled because they have something that they are unable to use effectively then they misuse it and make themselves seem even odder and it may interfere with other ways of functioning which they have developed themselves in order to cope. A good example is the injunction that is often given to children with Asperger's Syndrome, which is to 'look at me when I'm talking to you'. Children with Asperger's Syndrome, often if they look at you when you are talking, they feel as they are being penetrated by your eyes. It's very hard from them to control their levels of arousal. Partly, we think, because they miss out on a lot of their early social interaction through which babies learn to do this. So when they have direct eye contact they get a big upshoot of levels of arousal and that can distort all their other capacities to take in information. While they are looking at you, they may not be able to hear you. By forcing them to look at you instead of looking at a blank ceiling, which will enable them to listen to you, you are in fact destroying their capacity to listen effectively.

That is not to say that we don't teach the meaning of looking, that we don't help them to understand what looking is about but we help them recognise eye contact as a social signal. A social signal that they can give to indicate that they are listening but that they can only give if they understand the purpose and then it can become easier. So we teach them meaning, we teach them to recognise the social signals like eye contact and when to use them. Trying to force the issue before they understand can actually destroy what we are trying to achieve. Once they have understood what eye contact is it may still be difficult for them and they may need to take a more pragmatic view so that as they get older, they get to teenage level and perhaps the man wants a girlfriend, then we have to say 'well, if you want a girl, you will have to learn to look at her because otherwise she won't know you're interested. If they want a job we have to say 'Well, you'll have to look at them, at the person who's interviewing you otherwise they will think that you are shifty and not to be trusted'. You may even be able to say about one of their teachers 'When Mr Brown is talking to you, perhaps you can look at him now and then because he doesn't really understand about Asperger's Syndrome it makes him angry and cross when you are not looking'. You have a duty to help them understand how other people are going to interpret and deal with their behaviours. We can't expect them to take on too much at once and they have to be able to understand first before they can then adapt and make adjustments for our lack of understanding and adaptability.

3. Flexibility and social imagination

The third area is a confusing area. Some formulations of the triad will even see two areas placed in this third position so in fact there are four aspects to the triad which people with Asperger's Syndrome find very amusing. The problem is that in some formulations it is still referred to as imagination although Lorna Wing talked about social imagination. That's an important distinction, as children with Asperger's Syndrome especially can readily learn to do things like play at being Batman. What they can't do is play at being Batman and Robin because that means incorporating someone else's imagination into your game. They may also have some problems with imagination, not a lack of imagination. In my experience it is never a lack of imagination, in fact I have known many people with Asperger's Syndrome to have high levels of imagination including creating imaginary cities and composing and doing maths and writing poetry. In many aspects they can achieve in terms of imagination but often there are difficulties in understanding fully the difference between imaginary and real, especially when they are young. So they can become disturbed, more disturbed than other children by imaginary threats.

This is particularly apparent in things like dreams. I think it's because they miss out on that social learning, perhaps to understand the difference between what's a dream and what's real. We can all have a very vivid dream and wake up and for a moment or two we have this awful feeling that it's true but very quickly we can reality test, we have ways of finding out 'no, no, that was a dream' although if it's very disturbing we may still check. I've been known to phone my daughter to find out that she didn't fall over the cliff as I had dreamt that she had the night before. But when a young child has a bad dream and wakes up crying, mum or dad can come and comfort them. They can make the child feel better and they can talk to the child. Tell the child not to worry, that it was just a dream and that it's alright now and mummy's here. So the child can feel safe and secure again and go back to sleep. For a child with Autism or Asperger's Syndrome waking up in the night with a bad dream, they are not able to accept that comfort from mum or dad. They are unable to articulate what has happened and so they are not able to have the experience of getting that explanation. Instead of which, a fear of dreaming can build up so that some children with Asperger's Syndrome are either very disturbed all through the next day about some terrible dream that they have had and aren't telling anyone or scared to go to bed at night because of the dreams that they may have. There are other reasons why they may have sleep disturbances.

There are biological reasons why there are sleep disturbances in all the autism spectrum disorders but dealing with the aspect of dreams is a very real one. When I think of, rather than dwelling on this imagination which can be very misleading because the child who is then engaged in imaginary play either has their play downgraded by those watching or they are assumed not to have Autism or Asperger's

Syndrome. I think what's much more important and much more relevant in understanding people with Asperger's Syndrome and in dealing with it is to think of that area as being related to rigidity in thinking and behaviour because that is what is much more common. We know that all people with Asperger's Syndrome will have great difficulty in being flexible both in terms of what they are thinking but also when translated into their behaviour.

The thing about the triad of impairments is that the behaviour manifestations are going to be very different, they are going to vary according to the intelligence and the interest and the experience of the child involved. We must remember that the child with Asperger's Syndrome although they won't have a language problem as such and they won't have a general learning disability as such, they may well have other difficulties that may impinge. They might well have dyslexia for example or dyspraxia or hyperactivity or an attention deficit. Whether those other difficulties are worth separate diagnosis, co-morbidity as it's described, or whether in fact we can say that this area which involves so much of those difficulties in being flexible and adjusting to the environment can encompass many of the same areas that are common to these other disabilities, is a matter of choice but the problems are real and our understanding that the problems should be real so they might have other problems, they have these three areas of difficulty but because they are developmental they have them all together so it's not just additive, not just that they have communication problems, they have social problems, they have flexibility problems it's that they have all three and these things interact. One of the things that make us flexible, for example, is other people. Left to ourselves we all become a little inflexible. We do things on our own routines; we do things to suit ourselves. It's other people that interfere and make us adjust and show us new insights and help us make new connections and develop us in new ways. For most of us, those compensations of what other people do for us are worth what we give up in terms of organising the world to suit ourselves. For people with Asperger's Syndrome that's not true but beyond that, they don't have the capacity or the understanding, especially when young, to take on board other people's ways of interfering. They just become frightening and disturbing. So they develop then their own ways of understanding the world and their own capacities in trying to move it on.

All teachers will meet students with Asperger's Syndrome

Some of these people will be in mainstream classes, some will not. They are sometimes diagnosed sometimes not. We are dealing with children in all kinds of schools. Children with Asperger's Syndrome, because they haven't got a general learning difficulty, because they have language are most commonly going to be found in mainstream schools. Because we know that Autism is not longer regarded as a rare disorder especially in the form of Asperger's Syndrome, we know almost all schools will have some child with Asperger's Syndrome. All teachers will come across a child with Asperger's Syndrome in their class at some point at least. Of course, the child may not always have a diagnosis and this is especially true of Asperger's Syndrome because they haven't got the obvious things that often send them for a diagnosis like a lack of speech.

Early years

When they are little sometimes parents and others will think that they have a little genius because their language development is precocious. They are using very grown up terms, they are not using baby language. Often they can be articulating very clearly. The motor milestones may be perfectly normal although sometimes they can be clumsy but there are no clear indications that the child has an abnormality and parents may quite reasonably believe that their child is behaving slightly oddly with his peers because he's so bright, because he's interested in such grown up things like how the television works or the moon and the stars.

So when they come into school it is often the first time that others begin to judge them in relation to their peers. It may be the first time that people will begin to suspect that there is a problem. But even then as we've seen, may be the problem will be misread as something to do with a behaviour problem. Maybe people will think that they have been socially isolated, that maybe something bad has happened to them. Parents have often suffered in the past because of the difficulties their children show being contributed to parenting, and we know that is not so, parents do not cause Asperger's Syndrome. Of course, parents find it very difficult as we all would, to parent a young child with Asperger's Syndrome and over time the relationship may appear very strained and odd but that's because the parent is responding to the difficulties not creating them. So we have a child in a mainstream school where they may be coping with some aspects of lessons but increasing where other children as well as teachers are beginning to pick out that there are problems.

Diagnosis and labels

When they are very little, people are often anxious not to label a child, or perhaps not at all. The whole issue of whether a diagnosis makes a difference raises its head. We have to be very clear about what a diagnosis does. A diagnosis is not the same as a special need, of course not; there are many other factors that determine children's special needs. If you were disabled in special needs purely in academic terms many children with Asperger's Syndrome wouldn't have them although some still would because of other difficulties or they may develop them because they are not able to learn in the way that we decide that they should. But at the beginning they may not have special needs in an academic sense so why then would we need a diagnosis? It's just because the way that they develop is different and we're not prepared for that difference, so just as we spoke about in language, if a child is not responding in the way to our commands perhaps, if a child appears to be rude or being insolent because they are not obeying exactly or they are answering back or they are speaking to us with the deference that we think we deserve, using the same tones with their peers in the playground and getting ridiculed and bullied then without a diagnosis to make sense of that we actually slip in to other labels. It's not a case of 'to label' or 'not to label' because us human beings we're a categorising animal. We can't live without categories; we can't cope with the amount of bits of information coming into us unless we put them into manageable categories. It's only if we have Autism or Asperger's Syndrome that that process may break down, we have difficulty making those categories because normally developing individuals, we do make those categories and if we don't know what makes sense we'll find that the child with Autism or Asperger's Syndrome will have labels but labels like lazy, rude, disobedient, stupid, aggressive, all those labels which are pejorative and I suggest they're more pejorative than Asperger's Syndrome. Plus, they mislead us. If we act on the fact that we think the child is lazy or rude or disobedient or whatever we have said, it's not just that we are not doing the child any justice, we are actually not liable to produce effective ways of helping the child, with moving the child on. It's only when we come to look at them through the understanding that they may have Asperger's Syndrome that we begin to understand what we might do about it.

Lack of guile or deceit

In fact calling a child or imagining that a child is a liar or is deceiving us in some way is often to assume a capacity that just doesn't exist or is very hard for it to exist in Asperger's Syndrome. It actually takes a lot of social skill to deceive another person, a lot of social understanding, which is even more important and people with Autism or Asperger's Syndrome don't have that. In fact, one of their attractive qualities is this lack of that, the fact that they are easily set up by other children to do naughty things, but of course are easily discovered to be doing that because they will admit to what they are doing. Not understanding that they should not do it or that they will get caught. That's not to say of course that people with Asperger's Syndrome cannot learn the behavioural way to deceive. It's a bit like a dog. If you have a naughty dog that has raided the bins when you've gone out they can learn to run and hide under the cupboard when you come home. But it's such a transparent lie, it's so obvious that it's easy to know if the dog has been at the bin and people with Asperger's Syndrome are often capable of that kind of very basic behavioural deceit but not the kind with great malicious intent, not the machiavellian kind.

Theory of mind

There are often difficulties, particularly over homework or instructions for tomorrow like getting your ingredients ready for a cookery lesson, where apparently the child has not told the parents. But why? Have they just forgotten, is there some other deeper reason, like they don't want to do cookery? No. Usually it's because the person with Autism or Asperger's Syndrome doesn't understand that they can know something that someone else doesn't know, or equally that someone else can know something that they don't know. In the case of cookery for example, if they've been told to get certain things ready for a cookery session the next day they might well assume that the parents also have that knowledge. The same thing can apply to homework. They may be told that they should do something but when they get home they would expect help from parents because they have no understanding that parents wouldn't know the context in which they should do things. Of course, they may have no idea themselves that the homework is supposed to relate to the context of the lesson. It may be a very isolated event unless the teacher has understood that she needs to help them have the clues from the lesson to understand what it is that they need to do when they get home with the homework. Many a frantic parent has been up until one or two o'clock in the morning desperately trying to do the child's homework, because the child desperately doesn't want anything to be wrong. Most children with Asperger's Syndrome can't bear to have a cross on their work; they will rub a hole in the page rather than have a bad mark on it. They hate anything disorderly, therefore for them it is very important for them that everything is exactly right and as it should be but they may have no idea how to make it so.

Sensory experience

We often talk about children, young people and adults with Asperger's Syndrome as being over sensitive to stimulation. That may be true but in a sense it isn't really the heart of it. The difficulty is not being able to put things in the background, not being able to foreground things that are important and put into the background things that are not. So that the feel on the clothes on the skin, particularly shoes, the sunlight coming in through the window, the background noises that most of us are not aware of until they are pointed out, the pressure of the chair on your bottom. All these things we can be aware of, we sometimes will become aware of them if they become particularly insistent, maybe we wear some uncomfortable shoes, our bra strap is slipping or we're wearing a scratchy jumper, maybe it's a particularly loud noise, maybe it's a particularly irritating noise like a scrape of a knife on a plate. Those kinds of things will irritate the nervous system of us all, but for children with Asperger's Syndrome; they have no capacity to block these things out, while they concentrate on what the teacher is saying or even what they want to do. Everything comes at the same intensity so it's as if they have just an 'on/off' switch and they can let in all in, in which case it maybe extremely painful and difficult to deal with or they can block it all out. Sometimes physically by blocking their ears and closing their eyes, sometimes by concentrating down very intensely on some obsessional activity or object so that the rest recedes into the background. But then it can be very difficult to get their attention from that position because they have quite literally switched off. Some do learn to gradually let more information in and the more meaningful the information, the easier it is for them to do so. But many will struggle with that throughout their school careers and beyond, and some will still struggle with the unusual and the non-meaningful for all their lives. The key thing is to try to understand what is going on because its not a deliberate choice, they are not kicking off their shoes to be a pain or a nuisance, defiant, they are not changing into naturists because they can't bear to have their sleeves rolled up for a messy activity. We need to think about ourselves in those situations.

Do we always keep our shoes on?

When we go home from work at night do we keep our shoes on when we want to read the paper? Do we never kick them off and tuck our feet up? Don't we find we can read the paper without our shoes on? In the same way, the child with Autism or Asperger's Syndrome can learn without their shoes. But they have to learn to conform, yes they do, because again they will then stand out, they will be teased, they will be victimised. But make it manageable, one thing at a time, not too much at once. If they are in a carpeted room, do they really need to have their shoes on? Why not let them get started on learning without their shoes and then put their shoes on when they go outside. Later, when learning is more familiar and they have developed some good habits for learning then maybe they can learn to cope with comfortable shoes and then maybe even stiffer ones. But we shouldn't over interpret what they are doing. We should take our sensitivity from the child in determining why it is difficult to manage with their shoes on and as for rolling up sleeves, well, do we ever really need to do it? We may be able to bully the child into doing it but will the child be able to concentrate in anything else with that awful feeling? I love my sleeves rolled up. I hate the feeling of my sleeves being down to my wrists but most children with Autism or Asperger's Syndrome cannot bear it. They are like the Princess and the Pea. They cannot bear the wrinkle in the sock, the wrinkle in their sleeves. If they need short sleeves then talk to mum and let's have something that can be taken off and reveal the short sleeves underneath or cover up the clothes. Don't persist with something just because it's not a problem for other children and somehow you've got confused with the notion that treating children equally meaning treating children the same. Treating children equally actually means treating children differently but it means giving them equal opportunities to learn, to be advanced and to be comfortable in learning situations. And, for each child, especially children with Asperger's Syndrome, that's going to be very different.

Teacher awareness and support

A brief discussion about the problems with Asperger's Syndrome can be making many teachers feel anxious about having such children in their class. I don't want to pretend that it is either easy and certainly not simple. Their needs are very complex and we need to develop complex skills ourselves in working with each child. Plus, of course, there's no recipe. I cannot tell you what each child with Asperger's Syndrome will be like, what will be a problem for them, what exactly they can do with each individual child because they will all be different. We have to learn to develop to strategies that might be helpful across a number of such children but we will have to adapt them for each individual child. In doing that, we will get things wrong. Everybody gets things wrong working with children with Autism or Asperger's Syndrome because of the complexity, because we need to adjust all the time, be sensitive because they are developing very different ways which we are not naturally accustomed to. Our natural instinctive reactions often are not quite appropriate but it's important that we don't feel that we are completely de-skilled. The very things that make us good teachers in the first place; the care and concern, the observational skills, the ability to listen and to learn from each individual are what is needed. That together with that framework of knowing where those Autistic or Asperger's like difficulties might lie. Everybody gets it wrong, there's no expert out there who gets everything right and doesn't make mistakes.

The good thing about people with Autism or Asperger's Syndrome is that they usually have very clear ways of letting you know that you've got it wrong and then we can start again. We can draw a line under that and think 'well, I won't do that again' but of course we may do something else. Life is not boring when you are working with children with Autism or Asperger's Syndrome but it is very important what you do and attitude is as important as skills and knowledge because just being on the side of the child, just understanding that we have a child here with difficulties which certainly he or she may not understand but you may not understand immediately but together you can often find a solution if you are willing enough to try. It's only when we have an attitude that everybody must conform, when we are too scared to try and be more flexible because when we look at people with Asperger's Syndrome we actually look at ourselves when we are frightened. They are frightened of us because they can't predict us, because they don't understand about people. We become very scary because they don't know what we'll do next and it's very hard for them to judge. But, of course, when we look at children with Asperger's Syndrome we feel exactly the same. We too are scared because it's very hard to predict what they'll do next. We are scared that we may not be able to control it, manage it, and so we too become inflexible and tense unless we manage to recognise what's happening to us and step back from it and try to allow ourselves to fail sometimes. We know that it's only if we try for that adaptability that we'll actually manage to succeed in the end.

Physical development

Many children with Autism and with Asperger's Syndrome in particular have an associated physical difficulty. Sometimes it is of the dyspraxic kind which means that they can't control their voluntary movements. The planning and the execution of things that they do spontaneously is OK because that is triggered by the environment. For example, if you see a glass of water and you're thirsty, you can pick it up and drink it, no problem. But what if the teacher comes along and tells you to pick it up and drink it? Now you have to think about what you are doing, you have to plan that movement and that's where the problem is. So now it is very hard for that child to pick up the glass and drink it. But what if you don't understand the child's difficulty? Well then it looks very much like, 'well, she can do it when she wants to but she can't do it now'. It looks like disobedience, it looks like non-compliance. Many children with dyspraxic problems get into trouble for those very reasons, when in fact they are not able to help it.

There may be some form of Ataxia, which means that they are very clumsy, very wobbly on their feet, find it hard to establish their balance. Maybe they will be helped a lot if they can have their feet anchored when they are sitting at their desks. Many children with Autism or Asperger's Syndrome can't write very well because they are so busy balancing themselves because their feet are not properly anchored. Or it may be so difficult for them that they cannot walk on uneven surfaces and that may mean not just that they can't walk along the bars in PE but that they can't walk on grass or on sand and again, too often it's interpreted as a behavioural problem when actually it's very scary for them because their balance is disturbed by just that amount of unevenness in the surface. We also have children with Asperger's Syndrome who are very floppy and therefore able to extend their joints and many children can enjoy the notoriety this gives them in being able to seemingly dislocate their shoulder, bend their elbow back so that it touches their shoulder blade at the back, bend their fingers back to that they touch the wrist. Now you can think that all this is all some kind of party trick, indeed many children with Asperger's Syndrome use it as a way of trying to get into a friendship group by showing off these amazing skills but of course they are not skills they are actually signs of a problem and that same problem means that they can't hold their pencil, or they can begin to hold their pencil but it requires a tremendous amount of concentration and effort which they can't sustain. So after a while of neat handwriting it eventually goes to pieces. Again, without understanding, this is often interpreted as the child not trying, they can do it when they try but they are not doing it now. So this problem can often be solved or partially solved by using IT, using ways in which the child can have access to ways that are not so tiring in terms of making their response in doing their writing. This can only happen if we can understand where the child's difficulty is, so again, we need to be alert to signs that the child is having these kind of difficulties and we need to seek help from occupational therapists, physiotherapists or at least GP's for a referral.

Savants

One common characteristic with children and people with Asperger's Syndrome is that they have particular obsessional interests. They can become interested in things to an extraordinary degree and sometimes they can develop skills in that area, which are quite remarkable. Often they are so remarkable that we refer to them as 'savant' skills. Now, in a true definition, a savant is someone that has skills which are not only out of keeping with the rest of their development but are remarkable when compared to normal development. So it is not just that you are surprised that this child can do this but that it is amazing that any child can do this. Some of those skills are fairly common. A thing like a perfect pitch, if that's a skill, is very common among the autistic spectrum. Nevertheless, it's very rare to have somebody who can listen to a Sonata for the first time and just play it. That's a very rare ability. So if you have someone with Asperger's Syndrome in your class it is quite likely that they might have perfect pitch, that they might be disturbed by the singing of the other children that they don't match the standards that they set for themselves. That they might only want to sing when they are by themselves, so they find it hard to join in with others, but in other aspects their musical skills are not that remarkable.

Only very occasionally would you get someone with these truly savant skills. Teachers are then often concerned about how they should treat that. Should they allow the child to develop those skills? Should they try to make the child have more even development so that they help them concentrate on other areas? While there isn't a simple answer, I think that we do need to try and develop all aspects of all children, whether they have Asperger's Syndrome or not. If it affects an area of interest, a savant skill is going to be something that we can use to develop the child in other ways than in that particular area. Some of you will be aware of Stephen Wiltshire who is a savant artist. He hasn't got Asperger's Syndrome he has Autism with learning difficulties but nevertheless, his artistic ability is extraordinary. That was developed far in excess of his other skills and areas of development. Was that a good thing? Well, it has meant that to date he has been able to make a living, he's been able to pay for some of the help that he still needs in order to live. We have to be careful. Some of the things that people with Autism or Asperger's Syndrome can do, some of there savant skills become what we call 'so what' skills. Joseph Sullivan's (the character that the film 'Rainman' was largely based on) mother describes very well what a 'so what' skill is. Her son hasn't Asperger's Syndrome but he is reasonably high functioning with Autism. When he was little he could do many things including 100 piece jigsaw puzzles upside down, naming all the states in America where he lives, being able to spell them all before he went to school. Many things like this he could do. And at one of the early parent support groups his mother attended she was boasting about all these things that her son could do. One of the other mothers turned and said to her 'So what?' and she realised that that actually was right. He may be able to do all those things but so what? How could they be developed? He still had very many difficulties in very many areas.

I was in a mainstream school a few years ago now, where they asked me to look at a nine-year-old boy. I sat next to him and he started telling me all about animals living in the desert. It was quite interesting for about ten minutes and then I realised that I was listening word for word to a David Attenbrough video and I didn't want to particularly stay there for however long the video lasted so I was trying, at various points, to bring him back to reality so that he would talk about how the animals were eating in the desert and I would say "Oh, and what do you like to eat Derek?' But of course, I should have known better. Every time I interrupted him he had to rewind his tape and start at the beginning. That is what savant skills are often like. It's remarkable of course that a little boy could learn a video like this but what could he do with it. It's like the little child learning to count. They can count to twenty, or perhaps only to ten, but they can't start at six because at that stage they need one to trigger two to trigger three etc. They need each little cue to trigger the next bit. That skill is a step but unless it develops it is fairly meaningless. It doesn't tie into any other aspect of knowledge; the child doesn't understand what he's learning. It's just a first step and we need to look at so called savant skills in that light. If we can use them, if we can think of situations where it might be useful, learning poems is one thing, learning to recite but of course without an understanding of poetry, without that understanding what they are reciting, it's a very limited use. Sometimes we have try put it aside, we have to say that this is a 'so what' skill and even in this area I have to start again. With Stephen Wiltshire, he went to Art College and he's learning to do things with his art that he never did before. He's learning about light and shade, he didn't have those contrasts in his work before. We don't yet know how that will affect how he draws. And certainly with Nadia, which some of you may have read or heard about, was again an extraordinary case of drawing ability in a young child. It became far less extraordinary as she grew up and developed other skills. In fact, as her language developed it seemed that her drawing ability diminished. I have certainly met many people with Autism and Asperger's Syndrome who had particular skills that looked outstanding and savant when they were little but by the time they were in their teens their skills hadn't improved or developed and they were no longer so remarkable. So we should celebrate children's successes, but we mustn't over read it. We mustn't expect all children with Asperger's Syndrome to display such peaks of ability.

We must celebrate children's savant skills as we would for any child. It is wonderful if they have these achievements and we can use it to increase their self-esteem and their relationship with other children. You can regard them as having a special ability rather than having a disability. But we must not assume either that all children with Asperger's Syndrome will have such abilities or that this level of ability implies more than it does. It may be a very narrow skill and it may be one that cannot be developed particularly or used in other areas. If we can help the child understand and develop the skill then that's good but we have to accept that we can't always do that and we may need to start again even in that area of apparent very special ability.

There is a very interesting study going on at the moment in America and in Australia where they are, I think through laser which sounds highly dangerous, but they are zapping out areas of the brain which they think are affected in Autism just temporarily and with normal developing people and during the periods where those areas of the brain are not functioning then we get the development of savant abilities. So people who never before had perfect pitch, who have never been able to write poetry now have that ability.

The implication is that we could all have savant abilities. It seems that it's to do with the focusing down, of not spreading out of the connections. If you can isolate certain areas of the brain functioning that doesn't involve others then we can manage more within those areas but then of course we can't use it to cross other areas. I would have to say that this is the very early stage of the research but with scanning they seem to show that that's what's happening in Autism. It's the isolation of areas of brain functioning that enables them to increase their ability in that area which of course makes it harder for them to generalise or turn.

Inclusion

In talking about children with Asperger's Syndrome in mainstream school there's often a problem about how far we should be expecting them to adapt to a mainstream context, which is after all why, they are there, and how far we should be adapting the context to fit them. There's no simple answer to that but we have to use, if you like, common sense ideas about what we should be doing. After all, if you have a blind child you don't say 'well the world in main-stream school is geared towards children who can see, so we're going to just pretend that you can and you're just going to have to fit in as best as you can'. Obviously we wouldn't do that, we would recognise it as cruel and inefficient.

But sadly that's the message that often goes out to children with Asperger's Syndrome. The world is not going to adjust for them and they are going to have to somehow adjust to the world. What's important is that we enable the child to begin to learn and we have to remember that that means they are coping with a very confusing and difficult environment and to begin with. We have to try to make it less confusing and more manageable for them. Of course, as they get older they move through the school environment then we can expect to develop in them ways of managing with more complexity and less adaptation. But we mustn't do things the wrong way round. We mustn't overburden them and therefore destroy their capacity to learn and then regard them as failures in adapting to the system before they even have a chance to develop those skills and abilities.

What kind of structures can we have in a mainstream school?

Sometimes it's about taking things away rather than adding special things. I don't mean that we want to see little children sitting in booths in the middle of a mainstream classroom but do they have to be sitting looking at a picture of something that happened two years ago when you want them to write about something else? Do they have to be sitting next to a distracting window or, when it's no longer their turn on the computer must they be expected to sit next to it and watch some other child using it? It won't be very surprising if they spend the rest of their time trying to help that child or at least work out what on earth he's doing. It's very hard for them biologically to ignore aspects of the environment and to concentrate on what they're supposed to be concentrating on. So it's very disturbing for them, for example, to sit facing other children and to be expected to pay attention to the teacher who may be standing behind them or to the side of them. That's why they do so much better when classrooms are more formally organised so that the space that they can occupy is very clearly marked and very safe. Hot-desking is not the favourite activity of children with Autism or Asperger's Syndrome. They need to know which bit of space is theirs and if they have to share their space then that needs to be worked towards. They are often better off with their own desk to begin with and then helping them move on to being able to share desks or tables with other children, or for limited periods of time. They are better off staring at a blank wall or a wall that indicates clearly what it is that they should do.

That structure is usually best in a visual form. That doesn't mean to say that it can't be written words, a list…it can be very appropriate if the child is reading. For the younger child, that may be in pictures or symbols. In a nursery session it may even be objects. The point of structure which we all need to some extent but which is vital for children with Asperger's Syndrome is that it should tell the child what to do, when to do it, where to do it, who to do it with and most crucially of all, when it's going to end and what's going to happen next. For many children with Asperger's Syndrome it's very disturbing not to know when things are finished. So marking the end, clear beginnings and clear endings to lessons or periods or activities are very important in Asperger's Syndrome. That doesn't mean to say that they can't have some unobtrusive ways of doing that but that kind of structure will help then in a variety of situations. Assemblies are often a nightmare for children with Asperger's Syndrome. But we can help them to manage without being sat on or allowed to run out and have people chase them, by helping them understand the structure and when it's going to end. Assemblies may vary but they usually have a structure so we can have a little clipboard that the child takes with them and it might say that at the beginning there's going to be some music, there's a little card with that on and then when the music is finished the child can turn the card over. It can just be held on a clipboard with a paper clip then maybe the headteacher is going to speak, then there's going to be a class display etc. It's like any of us faced with something that is fairly meaningless and where we are not that well motivated to persist in the activity. I have the very same problem when I'm faced with a day's housework. The only way I can get through it is to make a list. To make a list and cross it off, so the satisfaction you might otherwise get from doing meaningful tasks with clear ends – the awful thing about housework is that it keeps on having to be redone. So we substitute those satisfactions by the satisfaction of ticking off on the list.

Disturbance in adolescence

Children with Asperger's Syndrome can and do, and one hopes certainly will, improve. We have to remember that their Autism will not go away; it stays with them. What happens is that they develop skills for managing, skills for coping, maybe even skills for hiding some of their difficulties. Those skills themselves can help them reduce the anxiety associated with some situations because they have ways of understanding these situations and they know what to do in them. But, we mustn't fool ourselves into thinking that we have cured the Autism and that the person can now manage without help. The person remains vulnerable. Not least because as they get into adolescence, like other adolescents they often develop emotional problems because there are a lot of hormonal and biological changes which in the case of Asperger's Syndrome will be compounded by not fully understanding what is going on and therefore being disturbed and maybe even frightened by those changes. Plus, the very fact that we have been successful building up their skills and understanding of themselves and others often means that as they approach adulthood they become increasingly aware of their own differences. They may also become aware of the fact that some of the opportunities open to them are limited. They may become obsessional about wanting a girlfriend but still have great difficulty in achieving that goal. There's a lovely, and in most people's books, a very successful young man with Asperger's Syndrome who is now a lecturer in the university but in talking about his Asperger's Syndrome he will put up on his C.V. the fact that he was engaged to be married for a year. For most people that would be a source of sadness and hardly something that you would proudly put up on your C.V. but actually, of course, he's absolutely right. For him it was a major achievement. He hasn't yet managed to have a longer-term relationship sustained but he did very well to do that. He's right to mark it. But increasingly, because they get additional problems and there's nothing in Autism or Asperger's Syndrome that protects you from getting any of the other emotional disorders that human kind is prone to. But also because of their specific problems in becoming more aware of their difficulties, late teenage time is often a very difficult time for people with Asperger's Syndrome. They become very vulnerable to depression, anxieties often increase maybe after having reduced during the school years they can come to the fore again during adolescence. They may revert to some much earlier behaviour – temper tantrums, but now of course they are 15, they are 16. A temper tantrum in a 4 year old is not that unusual and certainly much more manageable and far less frightening than a temper tantrum of somebody who is 15 or 16. They frighten others and they frighten themselves.

We desperately need to give them ways of coping, ways of recognising when they are getting agitated and disturbed and things to do to reduce that anxiety. Learning to relax – this is a great difficulty with people with Asperger's Syndrome. Having physical exercise to burn off those anxieties, to give them a 'jogger's high'. Helping them recognise the signal to others when they just need to escape. We can't always make environments so that stress is at a manageable level for them, but what we can do is train them to tell us when that's the case so that they can be given permission to leave and have some escape activity. So that, for example, there's a school where they have given a little boy a green ruler and a red ruler. They have taught him to recognise when he's becoming agitated, maybe he's begun to fidget, maybe his heart has missed a beat, maybe he's become hot. All these signs we need to notice and then help him notice so when he begins to feel like that, he takes the red ruler and puts it on his desk. When he's calm he has the green ruler. So that without drawing attention to himself or any unnecessary disturbance he gives the teacher a very clear signal that now is the time for her to intervene, to come and discreetly and quietly to suggest that he goes and listens to his music for a short while. To calm down and to come back. Teachers are often scared that if they allow children to escape from the classroom it will be hard to get them back. One can understand that fear. That's why it's important that we manage it. Mostly, if we are sensitive enough and help the child be sensitive enough to their feelings, the child will not abuse them if they know they can escape when things get too much they are much more likely to come back and to learn more effectively while they are there. So it's a worthwhile strategy to have in place.

Resources, Links and Organisations

General books

Attwood, A.J. (1998)
Asperger's Syndrome – a guide for parents and professionals
Jessica Kingsley
www.jkp.com

A general and practical book with lots of examples.

Cumine,V., Leach, J. and Stevenson, G. (1998)
Asperger's Syndrome; a practical guide for teachers
David Fulton
www.fultonbooks.co.uk

An excellent introduction to the subject covering assessment, educational and behavioural interventions and precision teaching. This is a very practical book with case studies to illustrate theory. An interesting approach to the case studies is the idea of looking at the situation through an 'Asperger's lens'.

Jordan, R. and Jones, G. (1999)
Meeting the Needs of Children with Autistic Spectrum Disorders
David Fulton
www.fultonbooks.co.uk

An excellent book which offers advice on each of the particular difficulties with practical examples.

Powell, S. and Jordan, R. (1997)
Autism and Learning - a guide to good practice
David Fulton
www.fultonbooks.co.uk

This book focuses on a number of curriculum areas and gives the reader insight into how to approach the subject and the benefits to the person with autism. Also included are sections on play skills, assessment and group work.

Whitaker, P. (2001)
Challenging Behaviour and Autism – making sense, making progress
The National Autistic Society
www.nas.org.uk

In this book Whitaker focuses on ways in which understanding and specific strategies can, combined with a knowledge of the child and the situation, be used to teach and support new ways of behaving.

Books providing personal insights

There are several books written by people with Asperger's Syndrome and a few are listed below. A specialist publisher of books on this topic is Jessica Kingsley and her website is worth a visit.

www.jkp.com

Jackson, N. (2002)
Standing Down, Falling Up – Asperger's Syndrome from the inside out
Lucky Duck Publishing
www.luckyduck.co.uk

A passionate and intense account of Nita's experiences during her childhood and adolescence. Nita is the lovely young woman speaking with various accents near the start of the video

Sainsbury, C. (1999)
Martian in the Playground – understanding the schoolchild with Asperger's Syndrome
Lucky Duck Publishing
www.luckyduck.co.uk

This book won the NASEN/TES best academic book award for teachers in 2000 and is a must for anyone working in the field.

Journals

A recommended journal is Good Autism Practice published by Bild Publications

Research

An excellent website for those who want to find out about current research and keep up to date can be found at
www.psychiatry.cam.ac.uk/arc/frames.html

Or contact

The Autism Research Centre
The University of Cambridge
Douglas House,
18b Trumpington Road,
Cambridge, CB2 2AH

Some examples of recently completed and ongoing research include:

- The early detection of autism in infancy
- The early detection of language delay in pre-schoolers
- Patterns of impaired and superior cognitive skills in people with autism and their relatives
- Family genetic studies of autism and language disorders
- Environmental influences (for example: obstetric or viral factors) as causes of autism
- Structural and functional neuro-imaging (fMRI) of people with autism and related conditions
- Early intervention methods for toddlers with autism
- The neuropsychology of Asperger's Syndrome
- The epidemiology of Asperger's Syndrome in school age children
- The association between autism and Tuberous Sclerosis

Useful websites

National Autistic Society
www.nas.org.uk.
The UK source for information, training and other links.

Tony Attwood is a clinical psychologist specialising in this subject and has his own website which is informative and user-friendly.
www.tonyattwood.com

Courses

There are many training opportunities to be found through links with NAS and schools of education. One headed up by Rita Jordan and especially interesting is described below. The information is taken from the home page
www.education.bham.ac.uk/programmes/ugrad/autism/web.htm

Introduction

This programme of study will be of particular interest to those working with children and adults with autistic spectrum disorders in the home, classroom or residential environment. Learning Support Assistants, Residential Social workers and parents will be among the people who will find this programme of study helpful.

The Qualification

The Post Experience Certificate (ASD) is a practice based programme of study completed over a year of study, earning 60 credits at level 1.

Subject to approval, students who wish it may progress to a full Certificate of Higher Education (ASD) for a further year of study. When completed the students will have earned a total of 120 credits at level 1 which could serve as a springboard for further, higher level studies.

The programme of study is designed to provide students with a broad understanding of ASD, an introduction to the latest research and an insight into current practice. It will prepare both practitioners and parents to draw upon recognised strategies to meet the needs of individuals with ASD in a variety of settings.

References

Aspergers, H. (1944)
Die 'Autistischen Psychopathen' im kindersalter.
Archiv fur Psychiatric und Nervenkrankheiten 117 p76-136.
English translation by Utta Frith (ed)

DfES, (2000)
Supporting pupils with special educational needs in the literacy hour
Ref DfES 0101/2000

Frith, U. (1989)
Autism and Asperger's Syndrome
Cambridge University Press

Kanner, L. (1943)
Autistic Disturbance of Affective Contact
Nervous Child 2, p 217-250.

Wimmer H, Perner J. (1983)
Beliefs about belief: representation and the constraining function of wrong belief in young children understanding of deception.
Cognition 13:103-28.

Wing, L. (1996)
Autistic Spectrum Disorders
Constable

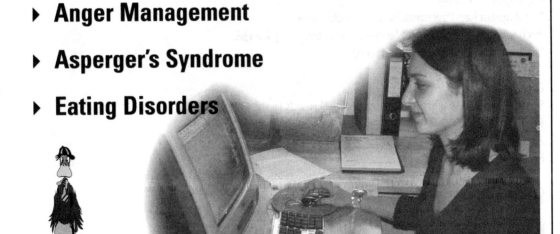